D0852088

Profiles of the Presidents

JOHN
ADAMS

★ ★ ★

Profiles of the Presidents

JOHN ADAMS

by Andrew Santella

COUNTY LIBRARY DISCARD TILLAMOOK, ORE.

Content Adviser: Caroline Keinath, Deputy Superintendent and Chief of Interpretation, Adams National Historic Site, Quincy, Mass.

Reading Adviser: Dr. Linda D. Labbo, Department of Reading Education, College of Education, The University of Georgia

J 921 ADAMS   17 95
Santella, Andrew.
John Adams

Compass Point Books
3722 West 50th Street, #115
Minneapolis, MN 55410

Visit Compass Point Books on the Internet at *www.compasspointbooks.com*
or e-mail your request to *custserv@compasspointbooks.com*

Photographs ©: Hulton/Archive by Getty Images, cover, 3, 11, 16, 21, 24, 31, 38, 50, 54 (right), 55
(top left), 55 (right), 56 (all), 57 (right), 58 (right), 59 (bottom left); Giraudon/Art Resource, N.Y., 6,
26 (bottom); North Wind Picture Archives, 7, 8, 12 (top), 15 (bottom), 17, 18, 20, 22, 23 (all), 26
(top), 28, 33, 34, 35 (top right), 35 (bottom), 39, 46, 55 (bottom left), 57 (left), 58 (left); Nancy
Carter/North Wind Picture Archives, 9, 54 (left); National Portrait Gallery, Smithsonian Institution/Art
Resource, N.Y., 12 (bottom), 48 (top); Stock Montage, 13, 14, 15 (top), 19, 32, 47; Fine Art Photo-
graphic Library, London/Art Resource, N.Y., 25; Library of Congress, 29; William Vans Murray by
Mather Brown, Andrew W. Mellon Collection, Board of Trustees, National Gallery of Art, Washington,
35 (top left); Department of the Treasury, 37; Maryland Historical Society, 40; White House Collection,
courtesy White House Historical Association, 42; Bettmann/Corbis, 44, 45, 48 (bottom), 59 (top left);
University of Rochester Libraries, Rare Books and Special Collections, 59 (right).

Editors: E. Russell Primm, Emily J. Dolbear, Melissa McDaniel, and Catherine Neitge
Photo Researcher: Svetlana Zhurkina
Photo Selector: Linda S. Koutris
Designer: The Design Lab
Cartographer: XNR Productions, Inc.

Library of Congress Cataloging-in-Publication Data

Santella, Andrew.
  John Adams / by Andrew Santella.
      v. cm. — (Profiles of the presidents)
  Includes bibliographical references and index.
  Contents: The "Ordinary Man"—On the Adams farm—The young lawyer—The Revolutionary—The
  first Vice President—Adams and his Cabinet—The Alien and Sedition Acts—War and peace—The
  President's house—The election of 1800—The legacy of John Adams—Glossary—John Adams's life at a
  glance—John Adams's life and times—World events—Understanding John Adams and his Presidency.
  ISBN 0-7565-0251-9
  1. Adams, John, 1735–1826—Juvenile literature. 2. Presidents—United States—Biography—Juvenile
  literature. [1. Adams, John, 1735–1826. 2. Presidents.] I. Title. II. Series.
  E322 .S257 2003
  973.4'4'092—dc21   2002003033

© 2003 by Compass Point Books

All rights reserved. No part of this book may be reproduced without written permission from the
publisher. The publisher takes no responsibility for the use of any of the materials or methods described
in this book, nor for the products thereof.

Printed in the United States of America.

Table of Contents

★   ★   ★

The "Ordinary Man"

★ ★ ★

It was Saturday, March 4, 1797, and every seat in Philadelphia's Congress Hall was filled. John Adams was about to become the second president of the United States.

George Washington was leaving office after serving two terms as the nation's first president. Washington had been the hero of the war for independence from Great

George Washington ▸
served two terms as
president.

John Adams stands to Washington's left as the first president of the United States is sworn into office in New York City.

Britain. He came from a wealthy Virginia family and wore fine clothes. He stood so tall that he towered over nearly everyone in Congress Hall that day. He looked like a leader.

Standing alongside Washington was John Adams. He was dressed in a plain suit. Compared to Washington, he looked short and stocky. Unlike Washington, he had not been born into great wealth. His father was a farmer and shoemaker from Massachusetts. Adams once described himself as an "ordinary man."

Adams may have thought of himself as an "ordinary man," but the times he lived in were anything but ordinary. Adams rose to the challenges of those trying times. He helped lead the push for American independence. He traveled to Europe to win support for the new United States among European nations. He served as the first vice president of the United States. Then, in 1797, he rose to the nation's highest office.

The "ordinary man" from Massachusetts had earned the right to stand among America's great leaders.

John Adams helped ▶ *gain America's independence.*

On the Adams Farm

★　　★　　★

In 1735, Braintree, Massachusetts, was a town of about 2,000 people. It stood along the shore of Massachusetts Bay, between the larger towns of Boston and Plymouth. Orchards and farms lined the road along the bay. On October 30, 1735, John Adams was born on one of those farms.

◄ John Adams's birthplace

John Adams grew up wanting to be a farmer, just like his father. His father's name was also John Adams. Besides being a farmer, John's father was a **deacon** of the First Parish of Braintree. He was also a lieutenant in the local **militia.** Also, the people of Braintree made him a **selectman,** a person elected to help run the town's business affairs.

John's mother, Susanna Boylston Adams, came from a respected family of doctors and merchants in Massachusetts. She was devoted to her family and to the local church. Besides John, she raised two younger boys, Peter and Elihu.

John's mother and father taught him to read at home. Later, he attended classes at a neighbor's house and at a small local school.

Years later, Adams wrote that his childhood had been "like a fairytale." He loved roaming the fields and exploring the creeks of Braintree. His days were filled with "making and sailing boats . . . swimming, skating, flying kites and shooting marbles, bat and ball, football, wrestling, and sometimes boxing."

When he was sixteen, John Adams entered Harvard, the oldest college in Great Britain's American **colonies.** It

was not unusual for students of the time to begin college at that age. At Harvard, Adams studied religion, Latin, science, and mathematics.

Adams graduated from Harvard in 1755. He tried teaching school for a few years, but he soon decided he wanted to be a lawyer. In 1758, he passed the exam that allowed him to practice law in Massachusetts. Adams then set up his own law office in Braintree.

▲ *Harvard University, in Cambridge, Massachusetts, was established in 1636.*

Abigail Adams ▶

John Quincy ▶
Adams, eldest
son of John
Adams and future
U.S. president

John Adams's young law practice often took him to Boston and other nearby towns. On one of those trips, he met Abigail Smith, the daughter of a leading family in Weymouth, Massachusetts. Like Adams, Abigail Smith loved to read. The two were married on October 25, 1764. They would have five children together. Their eldest son, John Quincy Adams, became the sixth president of the United States.

In the years ahead, Adams would have to spend a great deal of time away from home. He and Abigail wrote each other hundreds of letters over the years. Adams came to look forward to Abigail's letters. They helped him get through the trying times in which he lived.

The Revolutionary

★　★　★

In May 1765, Adams and other people in Massachusetts learned of a new law passed by the British **Parliament.** It was called the Stamp Act, and it placed a tax on newspapers, legal documents, and even playing cards. For the first time, Britain was directly taxing its American colonists, and the colonists were outraged.

▾ *Examples of the tax stamps that angered American colonists, including John Adams*

Adams believed that the Stamp Act was unfair to the colonists. He and other young lawyers from Boston led the

Boston colonists read the hated Stamp Act. ▲

protests against the Stamp Act. Adams argued that the tax was illegal because the colonists had not agreed to it. He pointed out that the American colonies were not represented in Parliament. The protests worked. In 1766, Parliament canceled the Stamp Act.

But that did not end the conflict between Britain and the American colonies. On March 5, 1770, a large crowd in Boston began pelting a group of British soldiers with snowballs and rocks. Some of the soldiers fired their guns into the crowd, killing five people. The tragedy became known as the Boston Massacre.

People in Boston demanded justice. The soldiers and their commander were arrested and put on trial for murder. Bostonians were so angry about the killings that no lawyer would accept the thankless task of defending the soldiers. Finally, Adams agreed to defend them, although he was afraid that taking the case would make him very unpopular.

Adams argued that the soldiers were only trying to defend themselves against a violent mob. The captain of the soldiers was found not guilty. Only two of the eight soldiers were found guilty of manslaughter, a lesser charge. Instead of making him unpopular, the trial earned Adams the respect of the people of Massachusetts. In 1770, they elected him to the Massachusetts **legislature.**

◀ *John Adams defended the British on trial for the Boston Massacre (top), but warned them of the colonists' rising bitterness against Great Britain (bottom).*

In 1774, Adams was one of five people chosen to represent Massachusetts at the Continental Congress in Philadelphia. The Continental Congress was a meeting of representatives of each of the colonies. It was called in response to the Intolerable Acts.

The first Continental Congress was held in Carpenters' Hall, Philadelphia.

The Intolerable Acts were laws passed in 1774 that limited the freedom of American colonists. Among other things, these laws closed the port of Boston and forced colonists to house British troops whether they wanted them or not.

In 1775, fighting broke out between the British troops and the colonists. At the Second Continental Congress that year, Adams pushed for the organization of the Continental army. He suggested that George Washington be commander of the army. He also argued that the colonies should begin building a navy. Most importantly, he urged the Continental Congress to declare their independence from Britain.

During the spring and summer of 1776, Congress debated whether to declare independence. Adams argued forcefully that the colonies must separate from Britain. He became a member of the **committee** responsible for writing the Declaration of Independence. Thomas Jefferson, future president of the United States, was also a member of the committee. He and Adams were friends. Adams knew that Jefferson was the man who could write the Declaration of Independence, and convinced him to take on the task.

Jefferson's eloquent words and Adams's arguments helped persuade Congress to adopt the declaration on

▲ *George Washington takes command of the Continental army.*

A committee of ▶
patriots, including
Adams and
Jefferson, draft the
Declaration of
Independence.

July 4, 1776. Across the new United States, Adams became known as the Atlas of Independence.

In 1778, Congress sent Adams to France to gain that country's support in the Revolutionary War (1775–1783). In time, France did provide military and financial support to the United States. This support helped the United States defeat Great Britain. Later, Adams played an important part in working out the 1783 **Treaty** of Paris, the agreement that officially ended the war.

◀ *John Adams, the U.S. minister, meets King George III (right) of Great Britain.*

In 1785, Adams was chosen to be the first U.S. **minister** to Great Britain. He left that job in 1788 and returned home. He had been in Europe nearly ten years.

When Adams returned, the United States was about to put a new system of government into place. This system had been laid out in the **Constitution.** Only a few months after his return, the first national election under the Constitution was held. George Washington was elected president, and Adams was elected vice president. Once more, Adams was being called upon to serve his country.

Two Parties Arise

★ ★ ★

Washington and Adams served two terms as president and vice president. One of Adams's jobs as vice president was to oversee meetings of the U.S. Senate. Whenever there was a tie vote in the Senate, Adams, as vice president, broke the tie. In such cases, Adams always tried to vote as Washington would have. He believed it was the vice president's duty to support the president's policies.

By Washington's second term, it became clear that the president's advisers

Vice President ▶
Adams

◄ *President George Washington meets with Thomas Jefferson (seated) and Alexander Hamilton. Jefferson and Hamilton eventually became political opponents.*

were splitting into two political groups. One group was headed by Alexander Hamilton, Washington's secretary of the treasury. These people were called Federalists because they favored a powerful federal, or national, government.

The other group was led by Thomas Jefferson, Washington's secretary of state. These people were called

Democratic-Republicans (or simply Republicans). They
believed that state governments should have more power.

The two groups split over foreign policy, too. At the
time, Great Britain and France were at war, and the
Federalists and Democratic-Republicans disagreed
about which country to support. Federalists wanted
friendly relations with Britain. Republicans wanted the
United States to side with France. As the split between
the Federalists and Democratic-Republicans widened,
the two groups became the first political parties in the
United States.

Adams was a
Federalist. In 1796,
Washington announced
that he would not run
for a third term as president. Adams then
became the leading
Federalist choice for
president. Jefferson was
the favorite of the
Democratic-Re-
publicans. Neither

Thomas Jefferson ▸

Jefferson nor Adams ran for the office the way people do today. Their supporters worked behind the scenes to win the election for them.

In the presidential election of 1796, Adams narrowly defeated Jefferson and two other men—Thomas Pinckney and Aaron Burr. Under the system used then, the person who came in second became the vice president. So Jefferson became Adams's vice president.

When Adams was sworn in as president, he gave a speech urging the country to rise above political differences. But his presidency

◄ *Thomas Pinckney, American general*

◄ *Aaron Burr, senator from New York*

would be marked by disagreements between Federalists and Democratic-Republicans.

Adams was the first president to follow another president in office. Today, it is normal for new presidents to choose their own **cabinet** members. However, in 1797, there was no pattern for a new president to follow. Adams decided to keep Washington's cabinet members. He believed that this would show his respect for Washington.

Adams's cabinet consisted of Secretary of State Timothy Pickering, Secretary of the Treasury Oliver Wolcott Jr., Secretary of War James McHenry, and Attorney General Charles Lee. Like Adams, the members of the cabinet were Federalists. But Adams found that he could not count on their support. Instead, they were loyal to Federalist leader Alexander Hamilton. Hamilton no longer held office, but he still had great influence on Adams's cabinet.

Secretary of War ▲
James McHenry

Trouble with France

★   ★   ★

The first problem Adams faced as president involved relations with France. France had helped the United States in its war for independence from Great Britain. Tensions between France and the United States had been growing for years, however.

France objected to a treaty the United States had signed with Great Britain in 1794. As Adams took office, it appeared the United States would be swept up in the conflict between France and Great Britain. By that time, French warships had even seized hundreds of American ships.

▼ *Two ships battle in one of the many encounters between the French and British navies.*

Adams wanted to defend American honor, but he did not want to become involved in France's war with Great Britain. Like Washington, Adams believed that the United States should not take sides in European conflicts. Still, he wanted the nation to be prepared in case of war. He warned Congress to prepare the nation's military.

Adams also sent three officials to France. They were ordered to work out a treaty that would ensure peace between France and the United States. In France,

Elbridge Gerry, one of the three officials Adams sent to France to secure peace

Charles Maurice de Talleyrand, French foreign minister who refused to meet with Adams's commission, resulting in the XYZ Affair

representatives of the French government told the men that they would have to pay for the honor of meeting with French government officials. Insulted, the Americans refused. This became known as the XYZ Affair, after the code names of three French agents involved.

Many Americans saw the XYZ Affair as a deliberate insult to the United States. They were outraged, and they wanted war. Towns all along the Atlantic Coast of the United States began preparing to defend themselves against a French attack. Their motto became "Millions for defense, but not a cent for **tribute!**"

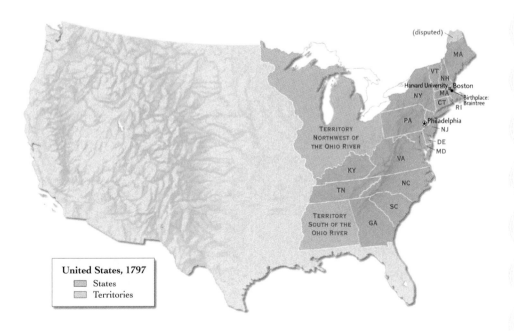

United States, 1797
— States
— Territories

Adams had long believed that the United States needed a strong navy to defend itself. Now he called for strengthening America's naval forces. Congress agreed and created a new Department of the Navy on April 30, 1798.

Congress also approved funds to create a temporary army of 10,000 troops. George Washington was called out of retirement to lead the troops. However, Washington was an old man by this time. It was expected that his second in command would be the real leader of the army. Adams wanted a Revolutionary War veteran named Henry Knox to be Washington's second in command. But members of Adams's own cabinet went behind his back and worked against his wishes. They convinced Washington to name Alexander Hamilton as second in command. Adams did not

General Henry Knox, Revolutionary War hero

trust Hamilton. He feared Hamilton would use the army to make himself more powerful than anyone else in the country, even the president.

Hamilton and other Federalists expected Adams to call for a declaration of war on France. However, Adams continued to work for peace while preparing for war. Both Federalists and Democratic-Republicans attacked Adams's policies during this crisis. Democratic-Republicans accused Adams of trying to start a war with France. Federalists criticized him for not declaring war. By trying to steer a middle course, Adams opened himself to attack from all sides.

▼ Though he distrusted Hamilton, Adams gave him the assignment of Inspector General of the Army in 1798.

By the summer of 1798, war with France seemed certain. Rumors of a French invasion of the southern states alarmed many Americans. Federalists in Congress reacted by enacting four emergency laws. Together, they were called the Alien and Sedition Acts.

Aliens are people born in another country. The Alien and Sedition Acts gave the president the power to **deport** the aliens if he judged them "dangerous to the peace and safety of the United States." Sedition means "encouraging rebellion." The Sedition Act made it a crime to publish "any false, scandalous, and malicious writing . . . against the government of the United States."

Federalists in Congress claimed that the Alien and Sedition Acts were emergency wartime measures. But Democratic-Republicans thought the acts were really aimed at them. Republican leaders such as Thomas Jefferson had hired newspaper editors to criticize Adams and the Federalists in print. The Alien and Sedition Acts would silence such critics. Democratic-Republicans also drew much of their support from people who had recently moved from Europe to the United States. The Alien and Sedition Acts would give Adams the power to deport these people.

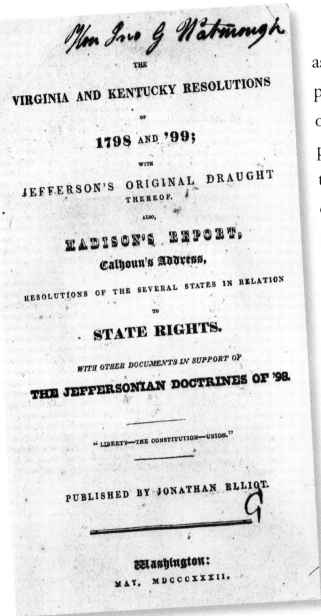

THE

VIRGINIA AND KENTUCKY RESOLUTIONS

OF

1798 AND '99;

WITH

JEFFERSON'S ORIGINAL DRAUGHT
THEREOF.

ALSO,

MADISON'S REPORT,

Calhoun's Address,

RESOLUTIONS OF THE SEVERAL STATES IN RELATION

TO

STATE RIGHTS.

WITH OTHER DOCUMENTS IN SUPPORT OF

THE JEFFERSONIAN DOCTRINES OF '98.

―――――

" LIBERTY—THE CONSTITUTION—UNION."

―――――

PUBLISHED BY JONATHAN ELLIOT.

―――――

Washington:

MAY. MDCCCXXXII.

Adams had not asked Congress to pass the acts. But once the acts were passed, he signed them into law. No other act of his presidency would anger the people so much. Most historians agree that the Sedition Act violated the right to free speech promised in the Constitution. The Alien Acts also gave the president complete power to decide who could or could not live in the United States. To Adams, the acts were needed because of the threat of a French attack. His

◀ *In response to the Alien and Sedition Acts, Thomas Jefferson and James Madison wrote and published these resolutions, which claim that states can, under special conditions, disobey the federal government.*

A cartoon shows ▲
the anger growing
between Federalists
and Democratic-
Republicans in
Congress.

critics saw them as dangerous, however. They gave the government new powers that took away some of Americans' most important freedoms.

Adams never tried to deport any aliens and, within a few years, the alien laws were no longer in effect. They never did much harm. But some Democratic-Republican newspaper editors were found guilty of breaking the Sedition Act. The laws became an example of how presidents must sometimes make difficult decisions during difficult times. They are also an example of how these decisions can have an effect on the freedoms citizens feel are fundamental.

The Alien and Sedition Acts were not the only emergency measures passed by Congress in 1798. On May 28, Congress gave the U.S. Navy the power to capture French ships sailing along the U.S. coast. This was the start of what came to be called the Quasi War between the United States and France. (Adams called it the Half War.) Neither the United States nor France ever formally declared war. Warships from the two nations fought battles at sea from 1798 until 1801, however.

As the Quasi War raged, Adams searched for a peaceful solution.

▼ *The American ship,* Boston, *battles the French ship,* Le Berceau.

John Marshall ▲

He had some hope when John Marshall returned from France. Marshall was one of the American officials who left France after the XYZ Affair. Marshall told Adams that in spite of the XYZ Affair, he believed France did not really want war. Adams decided not to ask Congress to declare war on France.

In the winter of 1798 and 1799, American ships won several battles with French ships. Adams saw this as his chance to win peace. On February 18, 1799, he made a bold move. He asked Congress to approve sending another American official to work out a deal with the French government. Adams chose William Vans Murray for the job.

Federalists in Congress were outraged. They believed that the president should be calling for war, not trying to win peace. Adams stood firm, however. He agreed to only one small change in his plan. Instead of sending only Murray, he agreed to send three people to France. The three were Murray, Chief Justice Oliver Ellsworth, and Virginian Patrick Henry. Congress had little choice but to approve his selections.

◄ *William Vans Murray (top, left); Patrick Henry (top); Chief Justice Oliver Ellsworth (bottom)*

Adams's actions cost him the support of his own party. Even his own cabinet members had objected to his attempt to win peace. Both Secretary of State Timothy Pickering and Secretary of War James McHenry favored war with France. When Adams announced his peace plan, Pickering declared that he was "thunderstruck." Adams could no longer put up with the disloyalty of his cabinet. In May 1800, he fired both Pickering and McHenry. He appointed John Marshall as the new secretary of state, and Samuel Dexter as the secretary of war.

Meanwhile, the peace efforts were proving as successful as Adams had hoped. The French government treated the Americans with respect. The French promised to call off attacks on American ships. They also agreed to allow American ships free access to French ports. With these promises in hand, the Americans signed a new treaty with France on Sept 30, 1800. Adams had won important changes in French policy without fighting an all-out war. He had kept the United States out of the wars between France and Great Britain. He had preserved American honor, too.

◄ *Samuel Dexter, who replaced James McHenry as Adams's secretary of war*

A New Capital

★　★　★

In June 1800, Adams led the government in a historic move. That summer, the entire federal government moved from Philadelphia to the brand-new capital city of Washington. The new city was being built along the Potomac River, which runs between Maryland and

Philadelphia in 1799 ▶

◀ *Washington, D.C., in 1800*

Virginia. Plans called for a beautiful city of grand streets and buildings. In the summer of 1800, however, Washington was little more than a sleepy village.

Adams arrived in Washington on June 3, 1800. He found only one finished government building. It was the Treasury Building. It would have to house the entire government until other buildings were completed. The

The final design for the President's House was drawn in 1793 by architect James Hoban.

new Capitol was not finished, nor was the President's House. (The President's House was not called the White House until after 1814. It was painted white to cover damage done by British troops in the War of 1812.)

Even though the President's House was not finished, Adams moved in during November 1800. His wife, Abigail, was still at the Adams farm in Massachusetts. On his second morning in the President's House, Adams wrote Abigail a letter. He said, "I pray Heaven to bestow the best of Blessings on this House and all that shall hereafter inhabit it. May none but honest and wise Men ever rule under this roof."

When Abigail finally joined Adams in Washington, she was shocked at the condition of the new house. She did the best she could with the damp, unfinished mansion. She even turned the East Room into a laundry room and hung the family's wash there. Today, the room is used for large, formal ceremonies.

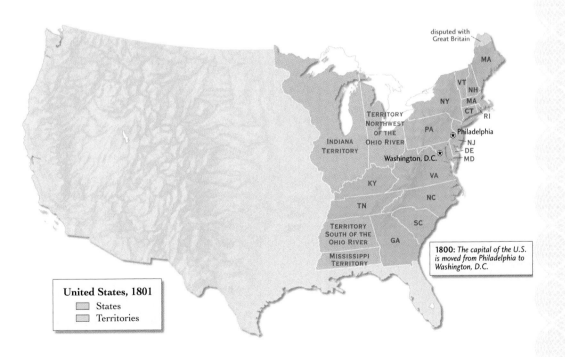

disputed with
Great Britain

MA

VT
NH
NY   MA
CT
RI

TERRITORY
NORTHWEST
OF THE   PA   ⊛ Philadelphia
INDIANA   OHIO RIVER   NJ
TERRITORY   DE
          Washington, D.C. ⊛   MD

KY   VA

          NC

TN

TERRITORY   SC
SOUTH OF THE
OHIO RIVER   GA

MISSISSIPPI
TERRITORY

United States, 1801
☐ States
☐ Territories

1800: *The capital of the U.S. is moved from Philadelphia to Washington, D.C.*

Today, chandeliers ▶
hang in the East
Room instead of
dirty laundry!

Going Home

★ ★ ★

In his four years as president, Adams had angered both Federalists and Democratic-Republicans. Democratic-Republicans attacked him for signing the Alien and Sedition Acts and for favoring a strong central government. Federalists were angry with Adams for not declaring war on France. As a result, Adams had little support during the election of 1800.

For the first time in U.S. history, the election of 1800 pitted a president against his vice president. Adams's vice president, Thomas Jefferson, was his main challenger for the presidency.

Jefferson was the favorite of the Democratic-Republicans. Adams was supposed to represent the Federalists, but some Federalists actively worked against him. Alexander Hamilton, for one, published a long essay criticizing what Adams had done as president. Of

President Thomas ▶
Jefferson, who
served two terms
in office

course, Democratic-Republicans also criticized Adams. Jefferson paid newspaper editors to print attacks on Adams. In the attacks, they made false claims that Adams favored a British-style **monarchy,** or that he was simply insane!

In the election of 1800, Jefferson and former senator Aaron Burr of New York each won seventy-three electoral votes. Adams finished third with sixty-five electoral votes. It was left to the House of Representatives to break the tie between Jefferson and Burr. House members voted to make Jefferson the third president of the United States.

◀ *Aaron Burr, who narrowly missed the presidency in the 1800 election, became Jefferson's vice president.*

John Marshall was ▲ chief justice of the United States Supreme Court from 1801 to 1835.

Adams was deeply disappointed in the results of the election. He felt that voters had forgotten his long service to his country. He also believed they did not understand and value the job he had done as president.

Still, he worked hard in his last few months as president. He continued filling government posts. One of the most important was his choice of John Marshall as chief justice of the United States Supreme Court. Marshall served as chief justice for thirty-four years. Some people criticized Adams for making the appointments, saying he should have allowed Jefferson to choose the men to fill these jobs once he became president.

Adams was sixty-five years old when he left office in
March 1801. He did not remain in Washington to watch
Jefferson be sworn in as president. He returned to his
home in Massachusetts, which he called Peace field to
commemorate the Paris peace treaty and because of the
peace and tranquillity he felt there. He never held
public office again. Adams and his descendants lived in

▾ *The Adams family
residence in Quincy,
Massachusetts*

John Adams ▶

Abigail Adams, ▶
famous as a
writer as well
as a first lady

the home until 1927. In 1946, it became a National Historic Site.

In retirement, Adams spent his days reading and working on his farm. He wrote a series of essays for local newspapers. He enjoyed exchanging letters with old friends all over the world. In 1812, in fact, he began writing friendly letters to Thomas Jefferson. The two former presidents became good friends again.

Most of all, Adams enjoyed spending time with his wife, Abigail. Adams's service to his country had kept him away from home for many years, but he and his wife were able to enjoy a happy retirement. Abigail Adams died in 1818.

John Adams lived to see his son John Quincy Adams elected president in 1824. But the elder Adams's health began to fail soon after that. He died at home on July 4, 1826, the fiftieth anniversary of the adoption of the Declaration of Independence. On his deathbed, Adams told his family and doctors gathered around him, "Thomas Jefferson survives." Actually, Jefferson died that same day, hundreds of miles away in Virginia.

Adams faced much criticism as president, but he could claim important accomplishments. He was the first president to live in the White House. He made sure the United States did not take sides in the war between France and Great Britain. He managed to keep the peace with France. In the process, however, he angered his own party and doomed his chances for reelection. Once again, Adams had put his principles ahead of his popularity. He once wrote to a friend, "I desire no other **inscription** over my gravestone than: 'Here lies John Adams, who took upon himself the responsibility of peace with France in the year 1800.'"

𝕸𝖊𝖙𝖗𝖔𝖕𝖔𝖑𝖎𝖙𝖆𝖓—EXTRA.

METROPOLITAN OFFICE,
July 12th, 1826.

Scarcely had the mournful intelligence reached us of the death of the sage and venerable father of our Independence, ere a fresh draught is drawn upon our sympathies, for his like venerable compeer JOHN ADAMS. *Jefferson* and *Adams* were twin stars that shone with resplendent glory, during the whole eventful struggle of the revolution. They have descended together to the tomb, and the prayers and blessings of their countrymen follow them. Their services, in conjunction with the happy coincidence of their deaths, have secured them an imperishable niche in the temple of fame. The late anniversary will be hailed as a glorious era in the annals of liberty, and we most sincerely trust will be 'solemnized with pomps, shows, games, 'sports, guns, bells, bon-fires and illuminations,' until the end of time.

It is our greatest gratification to record, that from the moment the melancholy tidings were received, every political feeling was banished; our citizens only remembered that these illustrious men were the promoters of their country's independence, and had hallowed it by their death. Indeed, if the world had asked a sign to prove the *divina origine* of our compact, it would have it in the *miracle of* their simultaneous demise, on the Jubilee of American Freedom.

The very day after our worthy Mayor had called the attention of the Town Councils in his truly feeling and eloquent address upon the death of Jefferson, he had to exercise his solicitude anew upon a like mournful occasion, which he did on Monday last, in the following words.

Mayors Office Georgetown,
10th July 1826.

To the Honorable, the Board of Aldermen and Board of Common Council.

Gentlemen: The Committee appointed by your honorable body, to adopt measures in relation to the death of the venerable *Thomas Jefferson,* met, and were proceeding with the arrangements to comply with your wish, when, this morning, it was announced that his compatriot, the venerable JOHN ADAMS, had also died on the same day. They deemed it respectful and decorous to suspend their proceedings until the Corporation should have an opportunity to express their sentiments in relation to this additional event, so well calculated to excite our feelings.

The character of the illustrious deceased is too well known to you, Gentlemen, and to his country, to render necessary any remarks from me; suffice it, that he was the efficient, energetic, and eloquent compeer of the illustrious *Jefferson,* and, in all that related to invaluable services to our country, his firm and faithful ally.

Very respectfully,
I am, Gentlemen,
Your obt. servt.
JOHN COX, Mayor.

Mr. Addison then introduced a resolution expressive of the high sense which was entertained by the Board of Common Council, and by every American, for the services of these compeers in glory, and a wish, that as in their lives they had been united in the great cause of liberty, so in their deaths the honors due their memory should not be divided. It is needless to add, that it was passed without one dissenting voice.

The Committee to whom was referred the necessary ceremonials, passed the following resolution:

At a meeting of the Committee of Citizens, appointed by the Corporation of Georgetown, for the purpose of adopting measures and making arrangements for paying all suitable respect to the memory of *Thomas Jefferson* and of *John Adams,*

PRESENT
John Cox, Mayor---John Mason---Walter Smith---John Threlkeld---Thomas Corcoran, Sen.---John Laird---William Marbury---Leonard Mackall---Clement Smith---Charles King---James S. Morsell ---Charles Worthington and Charles A. Beatty.

Resolved, That a day be set apart (of which due notice will be given) for the observance of such solemn ceremonies, as may evince the deep regret felt for the death, and the high sense entertained of the virtues, the patriotism, and the extraordinary usefulness during the long lives of these highly distinguished men—in which the citizens of the town and of the adjacent country of the district, and the strangers residing in the town and vicinity shall be invited.

That Francis S. Key be requested to deliver an oration on the occasion, at such time and place as shall hereafter be determined on.

That the members of this committee will wear crape on the left arm for thirty days, and that our fellow citizens be, and they are hereby respectfully invited to do the same.

JOHN COX, Mayor,
Chairman.

WALTER SMITH,
Secretary.

When they died, a special edition newspaper honored John Adams and Thomas Jefferson, patriots and presidents of the United States.

GLOSSARY

★ ★ ★

cabinet—a president's group of advisers

colonies—territories settled by people from another country and ruled by that country

committee—a group working together on a project

Constitution—the document stating the basic laws of the United States

deacon—someone who helps a minister in a Christian church

deport—to send out of the country by legal means

inscription—wording

legislature—the part of government that makes or changes laws

militia—an army of part-time soldiers

minister—an official who represents one country in another country

monarchy—a type of government in which a king or queen is the head of state

Parliament—the part of the British government that makes laws

selectman—a government official in a New England town

treaty—an agreement between two governments

tribute—a large payment demanded by someone with power

JOHN ADAMS'S LIFE AT A GLANCE

★ ★ ★

PERSONAL

Nickname:	Atlas of Independence
Born:	October 30, 1735
Birthplace:	Braintree, Massachusetts (now Quincy)
Father's name:	John Adams
Mother's name:	Susanna Boylston Adams
Education:	Graduated from Harvard College in 1755
Wife's name:	Abigail Smith Adams
Married:	October 25, 1764
Children:	Abigail Amelia Adams (1765–1813); John Quincy Adams (1767–1848); Susanna Adams (1768–1770); Charles Adams (1770–1800); Thomas Adams (1772–1832)
Died:	July 4, 1826, in Quincy, Massachusetts
Buried:	Quincy, Massachusetts

PUBLIC

Occupation before presidency:	Schoolteacher, lawyer
Occupation after presidency:	Writer for the *Boston Patriot,* president of the Massachusetts Society of Arts and Sciences and other societies
Military service:	None
Other government positions:	Member of the Massachusetts legislature; representative in the First Continental Congress; representative in the Second Continental Congress; U.S. minister to Great Britain; U.S. vice president
Political party:	Federalist
Vice president:	Thomas Jefferson (1797–1801)
Dates in office:	March 4, 1797–March 4, 1801
Presidential opponents:	Thomas Jefferson, Thomas Pinckney, Aaron Burr
Number of votes (Electoral College):	(71 of 276), 1796; (65 of 276), 1800
Writings:	*A Dissertation on Canon and Feudal Law, Novanglus Papers* (1774–1775); *Thoughts on Government* (1776); *A Defence of the Constitutions of Government of the United States of America* (3 vols., 1787); *Discourses on Davila* (1805)

★

John Adams's Cabinet

Secretary of state:
 Timothy Pickering
 (1797–1800)
 John Marshall
 (1800–1801)

Secretary of the treasury:
 Oliver Wolcott Jr.
 (1797–1801)
 Samuel Dexter (1801)

Secretary of war:
 James McHenry
 (1797–1800)
 Samuel Dexter
 (1800–1801)

Attorney general:
 Charles Lee
 (1797–1801)

Secretary of the navy:
 Benjamin Stoddert
 (1798–1801)

JOHN ADAMS'S LIFE AND TIMES

★ ★ ★

ADAMS'S LIFE	WORLD EVENTS
October 30, Adams **1735** is born in Braintree (Quincy) (below)	**1735** Swedish naturalist Carolus Linnaeus publishes his first work on botanical classification

1740

	1738 Englishman John Wesley and his brother Charles found the Methodist Church

1741 Germany's Handel composes his *Messiah*

1749 German writer Johann Wolfgang Goethe (above) is born

ADAMS'S LIFE

1750

Attends Harvard   1751–
(below)   1755

Begins practicing law   1758

1760

Marries Abigail Smith   1764
(below)

WORLD EVENTS

1752   Benjamin Franklin
performs his famous
kite experiment

1754–   The Seven Years' War,
1763   known in America as
the French and Indian
War, is fought; Britain
defeats France

1759   Author Voltaire of
France writes his
brilliant tale *Candide*

The British Museum
opens in London

1762   Catherine the
Great (right)
becomes
empress of
Russia
and rules for
thirty-four years

1769   British explorer
Captain James
Cook reaches
New Zealand

ADAMS'S LIFE

Defends the British soldiers involved in the Boston Massacre in court — 1770

Is elected to the Massachusetts legislature — 1771

Is chosen to be a member of the First Continental Congress (left) — 1774

Becomes a member of the Second Continental Congress — 1775

Serves as minister to the Netherlands — 1780

WORLD EVENTS

1770

1780

1770 — Five die in a street clash known as the Boston Massacre (below)

1777 — Vermont is the first former colony to ban slavery

1779 — Jan Ingenhousz of the Netherlands discovers that plants release oxygen when exposed to sunlight

1783 — American author Washington Irving is born

ADAMS'S LIFE

Serves as minister to Great Britain	1785
Is elected the first vice president of the United States	1789

The XYZ Affair takes place	1797
The Department of the Navy is established	1798
The Alien and Sedition Acts are passed	

1790

WORLD EVENTS

1791	Austrian composer Wolfgang Amadeus Mozart (right) dies
1792	The dollar currency is introduced to America

Presidential Election Results:	Popular Votes	Electoral Votes
1796 John Adams	None	71
Thomas Jefferson		68
Thomas Pinckney		59
Aaron Burr		30
Samuel Adams		15
Oliver Ellsworth		11
George Clinton		7
John Jay		5
James Iredell		3
George Washington		2
John Henry		2
S. Johnston		2
Charles C. Pinckney		1

1799	Napoléon Bonaparte takes control of France
	The Rosetta Stone, the key to understanding Egyptian hieroglyphics, is found near Rosetta, Egypt

ADAMS'S LIFE

	WORLD EVENTS

The capital moves from Philadelphia, Pennsylvania, to Washington — 1800

1800

Adams moves into the President's House

Appoints John Marshall (below) chief justice of the Supreme Court — 1801

1801 — Ultraviolet radiation is discovered

1807 — Robert Fulton's *Clermont* is the first reliable steamship to travel between New York City and Albany

1809 — American poet and short-story writer Edgar Allen Poe is born in Boston

1810 — 1810 — Bernardo O'Higgins leads Chile in its fight for independence from Spain

ADAMS'S LIFE

WORLD EVENTS

1812–
1814
The United States and
Britain fight the War
of 1812

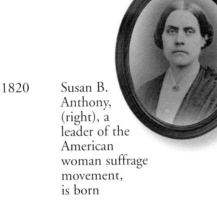

Abigail Adams   1818
(below) dies

1820   1820   Susan B.
Anthony,
(right), a
leader of the
American
woman suffrage
movement,
is born

1821   Central American
countries gain
independence from
Spain

1823   Mexico becomes
a republic

July 4, Adams (below)   1826
dies in Quincy

1826   The first photograph
is taken by Joseph
Niépce, a French
physicist

UNDERSTANDING JOHN ADAMS AND HIS PRESIDENCY

★ ★ ★

IN THE LIBRARY

Burgan, Michael. *John Adams: Second U.S. President.*
Broomall, Pa.: Chelsea House Publishing, 2000.

Lukes, Bonnie. *John Adams: Public Servant.*
Greensboro, N.C.: Morgan Reynolds, 2000.

St. George, Judith. *John and Abigail Adams.*
New York: Holiday House, 2001.

ON THE WEB

The White House—John Adams
http://www.whitehouse.gov/history/presidents/ja2.html
To read a biography and other information
about John Adams

Biography of John Adams
http://grid.let.rug.nl/~usa/P/ja2/about/bio/adamsxx.htm
To learn about Adams's life, from his childhood to
his political career

The Internet Public Library—John Adams
http://www.ipl.org/ref/POTUS/jadams.html
For basic information and links about John Adams

ADAMS HISTORIC SITES
ACROSS THE COUNTRY

Adams National Historic Site
133 Franklin Street
Quincy, MA 02669
617/773-1177
To visit eleven historic
buildings from five generations
of the Adams family

Burial Site of John Adams
1306 Hancock Street
Quincy, MA 02169-5112
617/773-1290
To visit the president's burial site

THE U.S. PRESIDENTS
(Years in Office)

★ ★ ★

1. **George Washington**
   (March 4, 1789-March 3, 1797)
2. **John Adams**
   (March 4, 1797-March 3, 1801)
3. **Thomas Jefferson**
   (March 4, 1801-March 3, 1809)
4. **James Madison**
   (March 4, 1809-March 3, 1817)
5. **James Monroe**
   (March 4, 1817-March 3, 1825)
6. **John Quincy Adams**
   (March 4, 1825-March 3, 1829)
7. **Andrew Jackson**
   (March 4, 1829-March 3, 1837)
8. **Martin Van Buren**
   (March 4, 1837-March 3, 1841)
9. **William Henry Harrison**
   (March 6, 1841-April 4, 1841)
10. **John Tyler**
    (April 6, 1841-March 3, 1845)
11. **James K. Polk**
    (March 4, 1845-March 3, 1849)
12. **Zachary Taylor**
    (March 5, 1849-July 9, 1850)
13. **Millard Fillmore**
    (July 10, 1850-March 3, 1853)
14. **Franklin Pierce**
    (March 4, 1853-March 3, 1857)
15. **James Buchanan**
    (March 4, 1857-March 3, 1861)
16. **Abraham Lincoln**
    (March 4, 1861-April 15, 1865)
17. **Andrew Johnson**
    (April 15, 1865-March 3, 1869)

18. **Ulysses S. Grant**
    (March 4, 1869-March 3, 1877)
19. **Rutherford B. Hayes**
    (March 4, 1877-March 3, 1881)
20. **James Garfield**
    (March 4, 1881-Sept 19, 1881)
21. **Chester Arthur**
    (Sept 20, 1881-March 3, 1885)
22. **Grover Cleveland**
    (March 4, 1885-March 3, 1889)
23. **Benjamin Harrison**
    (March 4, 1889-March 3, 1893)
24. **Grover Cleveland**
    (March 4, 1893-March 3, 1897)
25. **William McKinley**
    (March 4, 1897-
    September 14, 1901)
26. **Theodore Roosevelt**
    (September 14, 1901-
    March 3, 1909)
27. **William Howard Taft**
    (March 4, 1909-March 3, 1913)
28. **Woodrow Wilson**
    (March 4, 1913-March 3, 1921)
29. **Warren G. Harding**
    (March 4, 1921-August 2, 1923)
30. **Calvin Coolidge**
    (August 3, 1923-March 3, 1929)
31. **Herbert Hoover**
    (March 4, 1929-March 3, 1933)
32. **Franklin D. Roosevelt**
    (March 4, 1933-April 12, 1945)

33. **Harry S. Truman**
    (April 12, 1945-
    January 20, 1953)
34. **Dwight D. Eisenhower**
    (January 20, 1953-
    January 20, 1961)
35. **John F. Kennedy**
    (January 20, 1961-
    November 22, 1963)
36. **Lyndon B. Johnson**
    (November 22, 1963-
    January 20, 1969)
37. **Richard M. Nixon**
    (January 20, 1969-
    August 9, 1974)
38. **Gerald R. Ford**
    (August 9, 1974-
    January 20, 1977)
39. **James Earl Carter**
    (January 20, 1977-
    January 20, 1981)
40. **Ronald Reagan**
    (January 20, 1981-
    January 20, 1989)
41. **George H. W. Bush**
    (January 20, 1989-
    January 20, 1993)
42. **William Jefferson Clinton**
    (January 20, 1993-
    January 20, 2001)
43. **George W. Bush**
    (January 20, 2001-)

INDEX

★ ★ ★

ABOUT THE AUTHOR

Andrew Santella is a writer living in Cary, Illinois. He contributes to a wide range of publications, including *Gentlemen's Quarterly,* the *New York Times Magazine,* and *Commonweal.* He has written several books for children on the history of America.

DISCARD

COUNTY LIBRARY
TILLAMOOK, O